DATE			

BRAINSELL

BRAINSELL

—

Intellectual Strategies for Making the Sale

—

JOHN CANTWELL KILEY, M.D., PH.D.

Lowell House
Los Angeles

Contemporary Books
Chicago

Library of Congress Cataloging-in-Publication Data

Kiley, John Cantwell.
    BrainSell: intellectual strategies for making the sale / John Cantwell Kiley.
        p. cm.
    Includes bibliographical references and index.
    ISBN 1-56565-010-7
        1. Selling.   I. Title.
    HF5438.25.K545   1993
    658.8'5—dc20   92-26569
                                             CIP

Requests for such permissions should be addressed to:
Lowell House
2029 Century Park East, Suite 3290
Los Angeles, CA 90067
Publisher: Jack Artenstein
Executive Vice-President: Nick Clemente
Vice-President/Editor-in-Chief: Janice Gallagher
Design: Judy Doud Lewis

Manufactured in the United States of America
10 9 8 7 6 5 4 3 2 1

For my esteemed sons-in-law

Roger Charles Kahn, M.B.A.
and
James David Conboy, M.B.A.

CONTENTS

—

Acknowledgments

M y friends and editors at Lowell House, especially Janice Gallagher and Bud Sperry, zeroed in on my manuscript, superbly edited it, and gave it a wonderful "local habitation and a name." I am immensely grateful to them for their care and expert attentions. Dianne Woo did the final copy editing with fine-tuning skill and Peter Hoffman shepherded the manuscript through various stages of production and I wish to thank them. My literary agent, Dorris Halsey, was her usual indispensable self, and I owe her my sincere gratitude and wish to express my admiration for her. Joyce Howard read the manuscript and offered important criticism and encouragement. I wish to acknowledge encouragement and good advice from David Balding of Portland, Oregon. John Duncan Ryan, an Oregon attorney in the mold of Sir Thomas More, helped me in diverse ways, and I despair of being able ever to repay him. My two darling daughters, Therese and Rebecca, were unfailingly supportive of me both with their review of the manuscript and in every other way. They also provided me with three cunning granddaughters, and two brilliant, hard-working sons-in-law, to whom I dedicate this book.

God guard me from those thoughts men think
In the mind alone;
He that sings a lasting song,
Thinks in a marrow-bone.

—William Butler Yeats

BRAINSELL

Introduction

—

THE BLOSSOM AND THE THORNS

—

Mahatma Gandhi once said that a rose needs no publicity agent—which means, presumably, that it is able to sell itself, thorns notwithstanding.

About this a number of observations need to be made.

First, every product has something going for it (the "blossom") and something going against it (the "thorns").

Successful salespersons are those who sell their products by expertly calling attention to the blossom instead of hiding the thorns through deception. The thorns are always there as a negative factor, with their potential to ruin the sale, but they remain latent.

Second, successful salespersons are able to bypass the "thorns" that are attached to the selling profession itself.

It is not just the used-car salesman that many people don't trust; it is "anybody trying to sell me something." This mistrust prevails despite the fact that selling is honorable work. Even more, it is the bedrock on which the American way of life rests. The Declaration of Independence, for example, had to be sold to some very reluctant British subjects who were putting their lives on the line with their signatures.

Many potential customers fixate on the selling profession's thorns rather than on the blossoms it is capable of delivering. This is because salespeople have often sold a "bill of goods" to buyers who neither wanted nor needed it and who in many cases could not afford it. This has happened often enough for salespeople to be unwelcome at the door, whether it be at home or at the office, in the mailbox or on the telephone.

The thorns that now attach to selling complicate the lives of salespersons.

On this point, two further things need to be said: (1) it is the nature of the human mind to "see" categories first. "Salesperson" is a category and, for many Americans, an untrustworthy category; and (2) it is also the nature of the human mind to be able to get past categories and to *see* the individual. That is why getting into the house is so important in selling. It is often the only chance of making the sale.

There is little that the individual can do about the stigma attached to the category of salesperson. It is probably a permanent thorn that complicates the work of the selling professional.

But there is something that the salesperson can do to minimize the hazards connected with this human trait of categorizing and even to use it to his or her advantage.

The human mind ultimately grows weary of categorizing. To drop a mind-set, even temporarily, is refreshing to the human spirit, a true relief. Helping to shatter the negative stereotype of salespeople is akin to a surgeon operating on a blocked tube or vessel to the brain or heart, giving new life to a stifled or moribund part.

Successful salespersons know how to make themselves blossom in the mind of a potential customer despite the thorns, which may include those of a personal nature, such as lack of charm, personality, and good looks. They are able to sell the product's or the concept's blossom in spite of its thorns; sell their profession despite its tarnished image, and sell themselves despite any personal limitations.

This is not a task for simpletons. If success is the goal, every resource of intellect needs to be brought to bear on it.

Successful selling is a complex business. Its four primary truths help to simplify it and make the task of selling much easier. In this book I will discuss, illustrate, and analyze these four truths, which are the keys to successful selling.

Part One of *BrainSell* will focus on the first truth: that successful selling requires the creation of good will. This means religiously keeping your word to a customer. Doing otherwise is an act of disrespect and contempt for the customer and quickly destroys your most precious asset in selling.

The second truth, covered in Part Two, is that successful selling requires skillful self-management by deliberately making and faithfully keeping your self-promises. Failure to do so limits self-growth and involves you in acts of self-betrayal, with disastrous professional and personal consequences.

In the third truth, successful selling means staying in real time. If you do not remain contemporary, you will find yourself filling in the gaps with fabrications and evasions, leading to a loss of authenticity and credibility. This is the topic of Part Three.

Finally, in Part Four, the last and perhaps most important truth is that successful selling requires real self-understanding. This means, first, to be aware that your own consciousness is the all-important arena in life. Here and nowhere else occurs the self-talk that programs the brain. This talk occurs in a mysterious place, called consciousness, to which only you have access. This access means unique self-involvement, which is the root of your autonomy. You are completely in control of the on-and-off switches of your thinking and will power. Accordingly, blaming outside factors, such as bad luck, or other people, such as incompetent managers, for difficulties and setbacks cannot be an explanation for failure. I will address blaming in chapter 14.

There is abundant sales literature, available in every library and bookstore, on such important matters as prospecting, presentation, overcoming objections, and closing.

One can look long and often in vain, however, for books dealing with the strategies presented in BrainSell, strategies that have been called intellectual. Successful salespeople intuitively know and apply these strategies or discover them either by self-observation during their selling experiences or by self-replay later.

My belief is that the unabashed and unashamed use of the enormous and often unused resources of intelligence, in which selling techniques are backed by solid, applicable theory, can lead to immediate increases in sales and to an eminently successful career as a salesperson.

BrainSell will show you: (1) how to generate goodwill, an area poorly understood by many salespeople; (2) how to accomplish your objectives, which is often a simple matter of making and keeping your own self-promises; (3) how to achieve greater credibility and authenticity by avoiding evasions and fabrications and by learning how and why to stay in real time; and (4) how to overcome discouragement, depression, and feelings of inferiority and inadequacy (and worse states, such as self-contempt, despair, and escapism into alcohol, drugs, madness, and suicide) through self-understanding.

The core of self-understanding is to understand your mind and consciousness. Part Four of this book will carry the reader deeply into theory, making the approach of *BrainSell* rather unique in the literature of selling. In its own way, this part of the book could prove to be the most practical. (The best selling techniques won't work on a day when everything seems dark and gloomy.)

BrainSell was written for those who want to move into the charmed circle with those who are thriving, both financially and personally, in the sales field.

It may also be of interest to those successful salespeople for whom the strategies presented in this book are already second nature. These individuals may be surprised (and secretly pleased) to hear their time-tested methods of selling labeled "intellectual," and to be told that they have been using their brains more than their feet to make the sale.

Does this knowledge make them intellectuals?

When all is said and done, an "intellectual" is simply a human being who uses his or her brain to achieve a goal.

It means knowing how to sell the blossom despite the thorns.

And this is your ultimate intellectual strategy.

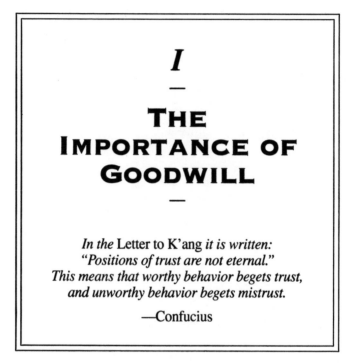

I

—

THE IMPORTANCE OF GOODWILL

—

In the Letter to K'ang *it is written:*
"Positions of trust are not eternal."
This means that worthy behavior begets trust,
and unworthy behavior begets mistrust.

—Confucius

1
—
THE SHAKEOUT
—

I t is not an altogether bad idea to copy the successful formula of the TV soap opera: Tell them what is going to happen, make it happen, and then tell them what happened.

What unfolds in this chapter and in the two that follow are—let me be honest—soap operas.

My intention is to entertain and thus capture interest.

The soap operas in this book, however, are not about a lover struggling through scary subplots to win his or her beloved, but about something almost as entertaining and important, namely salespersons achieving success despite the difficulties—the "thorns."

In this chapter we will meet Paula Rem, a successful real estate broker. She is successful because she knows what creates goodwill and has made that knowledge her personal and company policy.

What follows is a slice of Paula's life, a brief glance at her style and habit of doing business. We will see her promise to deliver a new house to a family under a crucial time constraint, and we will see that promise thoroughly tested.

◆◆◆◆

P aula reached for the phone on her desk and dialed a number. She heard it ring twice, and then a voice answered at the other end. "Hello."

"Mr. Tulip? This is Paula Rem of Rem Realty. I promised to call you back when I got a commitment from the builder."

"How does it look, Ms. Rem?"

"He assures me the house will be ready for occupancy by noon on Monday."

"Can I depend on that?"

"If I have to work him around the clock, Mr. Tulip, your house will be ready. I give you my word."

"Otherwise, Ms. Rem, I'd rather drop the whole matter and commit myself to another house I've looked at. As I have explained, I simply must be able to move my wife and children in on schedule. A delay is unthinkable for reasons that you know."

"I will move heaven and earth to get you in on schedule, Mr. Tulip. Leave everything to me."

"Well, I much prefer that house, as you know. But the other house is ready now."

"I have solid assurances from the builder. He is very dependable, and he hasn't let me down yet. Your house will be ready, Mr. Tulip. Put your mind at rest."

"I trust you, Ms. Rem. The movers will be at the front door by noon Monday. We will be with them. See you then."

Paula hung up the phone. She had less than a week to do what she had guaranteed. *Plenty of time,* she thought. Yet, it would have been so much easier to have sold the other house to the man. No hassle. No problems for a wife on a respirator who had to have things ready for her without fail. No second guesses. No alibis. *Yes,* she thought. The house the Tulips preferred was the right one to sell them. She knew what had gone into each house. Mrs. Tulip deserved the better one. God! Twelve years as a paraplegic, following an auto accident! The very idea chilled Paula. What some people have to go through in life. She felt a surge of admiration for Mrs. Tulip and for her husband. Then she visualized herself in the same predicament. A shudder went through her. She shook her head in an effort to dismiss the thought, then quickly turned to the business before her on her desk. She reached for the phone, punched the buttons, and waited for a familiar voice.

"Faron Construction. Miss Daly speaking. Can I help you?"

"It's Paula, Judy. Oscar in?"

"Yes. I'll connect you, Paula."

Paula heard a click, then a male voice came on the line. "Oscar speaking."

"Oscar, it's Paula. I said I'd call you right back. I've just passed on the message about the Tulip house. The man has committed himself to it, subject to its readiness by the day I told you, next Monday at noon. The fat is in the fire, Oscar. Everything is up to you now."

"Barring an earthquake, we'll have it ready. It'll mean pushing it, but we'll do it. Trust me, Paula."

"You're the only builder in town I would trust, Oscar, for a very good reason: you've always kept your promises to me."

"One of these days I'm going to disappoint you, Paula. I'm human, you know. But not this time. I'm pulling out all the stops on this one, given the circumstances. I really feel for that guy."

"If you run into a snag, major or minor, call me. Anytime, day or night. I'm tracking this thing like a moon shot, you hear?"

"Will do."

The two said good-bye to each other and hung up. It was now closing time. Paula looked first at her watch and then picked up a little calendar on her desk. It was Wednesday. There were two more working days. Should be enough time, she mused. If not, there is the whole weekend. It meant over-time for the workmen, but Oscar would absorb half the cost, and she would pick up the rest, if necessary. No problem, she reassured herself almost audibly as she threw the light switch and closed and locked the door behind her. Then she stood on the sidewalk outside her office and read the gilded sign on the big window: REM REALTY. Underneath the name was her motto: WE KEEP OUR PROMISES. Then she walked through the arched passageway to the parking area behind the building. She climbed into her car, started it, switched on the headlights, and drove off into the enveloping twilight. "We keep our promises," she whispered to herself.

The words lingered in her brain with special meaning. She thought of the brave lady on the respirator and her gallant husband, and of her promise to them. Could she keep it this time?

She drove the short distance to her house, oblivious to almost everything but her thoughts. It was, after all, a routine thing: getting a house ready for occupancy. Oscar had done it two dozen times before for her. Paula heard Oscar's words again as she pulled into her driveway. "Barring an earthquake," he had said. She stepped out onto the solid ground and then, impulsively, tested it with two small jumps in place. *Solid as a rock,* she thought and, smiling, went in to her house to greet her husband, Ben, and their children.

Paula felt the first rumble in the middle of the night. She woke up instantly, switched on the light by the bed, and sprang to her feet. Ben had felt it too. "Paula, it's an earthquake! Let's get the children."

The words were hardly out of his mouth when a terrifying noise, incredibly loud and clear, reached their ears. The whole house began to shake, and the floor shifted beneath their bare feet. The bedroom furniture moved as if pushed by a giant, unseen hand. Paula ran down the hall to the children's rooms. She heard their screams over the sound of falling objects all through the house. Ben was right behind her.

"Tom, Peter, Alice, come with us!" he ordered with a stern authority he rarely used with them.

Paula scooped her four-year-old daughter into her arms and tried to comfort her. The house shook again, this time more violently, and a more awful and stupefying noise reached their ears.

"It's an earthquake!" shouted Tom, with obvious delight.

"Awesome!" exclaimed Peter, taking up the chorus. The boys had read about earthquakes in school and at first had been excited by them until they learned how rare the occurrence was. "Rats," Peter had said one night at dinner, "bet we never have one." Now that the real thing had come, the boys couldn't have been more pleased.

Ben led his family to the front door, threw it open, and stationed everyone underneath the doorway. It was, he had read, the place safest from falling plaster and beams. Her heart pounding, Paula stood there holding Alice. Ben had his arms around their two sons.

Was this the end? Paula wondered. "Please God, no," she murmured to herself. Then the terrifying rumbling began to subside, and the house stopped shaking. "Thank God," Paula said softly. She started to move out from under the doorway.

"Wait, Paula. It may come again," said Ben.

Then it came again: an aftershock, feebler by comparison, yet still terrifying.

Paula hurried back to her husband's side.

"An aftershock," he said. "It'll pass. Let's hope so."

It did. The whole adventure had taken less than five minutes. Before another hour had passed, the children were back in bed and asleep and the house had been thoroughly inspected and found to have sustained little or no damage.

"Quite an experience," said Paula, as she switched off the bedside lamp for the second time that night. "Something to tell our grandchildren." She went into Ben's arms then, still quivering; whether it was from the chill night air or the excitement, Ben could not be sure. They lay together in the soft moonlight that invaded their now quiet bedroom. The stillness was magical.

"There's nothing like the noise of an earthquake to help one appreciate a little peace and quiet," she whispered to her husband.

Soon they, too, were sound asleep.

Paula woke up at first light. Something had troubled her sleep. Then, instantly, she remembered the earthquake. She thought she had heard sirens. Had there been loss of life, fires, the collapse of buildings? Ben was still sound asleep, and Paula got up for a tour of the house and found its contents in shambles. There was no structural damage to walls or ceiling that she could see, but books and china were all over the floors of the living room, den, and kitchen. She picked up a few things and righted a bookcase and a table. Ten minutes later she was dressed and in her car, heading for the Tulip house a few miles away and dreading what she might find.

The ride took her to the other house, the one that was ready but not "good enough" for the Tulips. Paula saw precisely how really "ungood enough" it now was. The earthquake had done thousands of dollars' worth of damage to it. She stopped and got out to get a closer look.

The building had literally been twisted out of plumb as though some colossal hand had grabbed hold of it. Paula could not believe her eyes. Could the quake have been that bad? One thing she knew for sure about the builder: he was long on excuses and short on performance.

Paula got back in her car, wondering how well the "better house" had fared—the house both she and the Tulips preferred.

By the time she reached the house her heart was beating wildly. Oscar was standing on the curb. Paula pulled up and rolled down her window. "I've just come from that other house," she said. "It's twisted completely out of shape."

"I'm not surprised," replied Oscar.

"How is this one?" Paula asked, afraid of what might be the answer.

"Came through with flying colors. No damage at all."

Paula visibly relaxed. "Are we still good for Monday noon?"

"Sure thing, Paula. We'll be out of here by four tomorrow," Oscar said. "Barring earthquakes, of course," he added with a smile.

Paula waved good-bye and drove home, Oscar's words resonating in her head. She thought of her company motto, WE KEEP OUR PROMISES, and whimsically wondered whether she should add the words, BARRING EARTHQUAKES. She promised herself to give it some thought.

◆◆◆◆

The Tulip family was able to move into their new home on schedule, as Paula promised. And if Mr. Tulip is ever asked to recommend a broker, wouldn't it be natural for him to recommend Paula Rem with enthusiasm? Didn't she earn his goodwill? Wouldn't he be able to say with conviction, "Go to Paula Rem. She really keeps her promises"?

Given the risks to his family, Mr. Tulip displayed great confidence in Paula Rem. He believed her when she said the house would be ready. Why? Was it because of a certain motto on her office window? Hardly. Mr. Tulip had too much at stake to take chances with "word merchants." He checked Paula out, and he was told by everyone that she would deliver, barring an act of God. He learned that she worked only with reputable builders, and that her business interfacing was rigorous and very selective. One person had called it a Goodwill Network. "Meaning what?" Mr. Tulip had asked.

"Meaning that you don't get a second chance to break a promise to Paula Rem," the person told him. "If you break any promise to her, you're dead in the water, as far as she is concerned. People are on their toes with her. She's a package. She delivers a whole network, not just herself." Then that person added, prophetically, "Only something like an earthquake would keep her from delivering; it can bring down the best of houses. Which is a good reason for a broker in earthquake country to know her builder—and if anybody does, Paula does."

2
—
THE DERELICT
—

In this soap opera "episode," we meet another person who takes seriously her promises made to others. Those "others" are anybody and everybody, not just people who can benefit her. Her promises are always "keepable"; that is, they are within her limited resources of time and the circumstances of the situation. Her guiding rule is this: no idle promises, and no promises she cannot—or does not intend to—keep. Her motivation? Simple helpfulness to others, because it is a good way to live. Does she target only those from whom she can personally benefit? Not really. But will there be personal benefit? Yes. In the long haul, she knows this will be the case. She knows—not just thinks or supposes—that making and keeping promises to others is the way to create goodwill. Does she need to enjoy the goodwill of others? Of course she needs to; we all do.

Let's meet the leading lady in our next melodrama.

◆◆◆

Claudia Adams was new to California. She had taken Horace Greeley's advice about the West and applied it to a career in real estate. So, after a couple of selling jobs, she finally came to rest at Rem Realty. Why this one out of all the thousands? She was attracted to its ad in the newspaper with the claim that "We keep our promises."

"That's for me," Claudia said, and the next day she went to the Rem office. Paula Rem was sitting at her desk when Claudia walked in. "Ms. Rem, my name is Claudia Adams. I'm looking for a job selling real estate."

Paula looked up from her pile of papers at the woman before her, judging her to be about 30 years of age. "Good. Please make yourself at home, Ms. Adams. I suppose you have a license to sell in the state?"

Claudia took a seat. "Yes, I do. Have you got an opening?"

"I'm always looking for qualified, hard-working people."

"I'm not afraid of hard work, and I've had about four years of selling experience." Claudia had deep-blue eyes set in an attractive face. She brushed a lock of dark hair from her forehead as she spoke.

"I'll need some references and some background information," Paula said, handing the woman an application form. Then she asked, "May I inquire what brought you to this agency in particular?"

"I like your slogan," replied Claudia truthfully. "It's different."

"Why do you think so?"

"It's bold. Spells things out." Claudia smiled as she spoke.

Paula waited to hear more. If she liked what she heard, and if everything else checked out, she might offer the woman a job.

"Spell things out? What do you mean?"

"Well, it invites the public to hold you to what you say. Explicitly. Not every person in business is willing to be tested that way. I know. *From experience.*" She flung out the last two phrases with considerable feeling. Paula took it as an invitation to inquire further.

"Sounds like you have a story to tell."

"Do you have time?"

"My work can wait a bit. I'd be happy to listen to your story right now, if you'd like," Paula said, leaning back in her chair.

"You may find this a little hard to believe, but it really happened," Claudia began, a faint smile still on her face. "It involves a piece of desert property and some promising."

Paula felt she knew something about promising. "Please go on. I'm interested," she said to the younger woman, who seemed to pause for permission to proceed with her tale.

"One day the broker I worked for, another agent, and I were on our way to Las Vegas to look at some ranch property that we had listed. I was driving. It was spring, but quite warm and very dry. We were passing through some very barren country, at about two in the afternoon, when an old man, stooped and bearded, sought a ride from us. It was in the middle of nowhere. He was just standing there in tattered clothes, no hat, holding out his thumb. We drove by him, and then suddenly I decided to pick him up. I had gone about a hundred feet past him, so I stopped the car and began backing up.

"'Think I'll pick up the old fella,' I announced.

"'What for?' Wanda, the broker, protested. 'He's a derelict. Probably got fleas, too. And he might be dangerous.'

"I continued backing up until I finally reached him. 'He's just an old man in distress. We'll just take him to the next town,' I said firmly. I lowered the rear window and said, 'Hop in, old timer.'

"'Thank you,' the old man murmured, climbing in and pulling the back door shut with a bony hand. 'I needed a ride badly and appreciate it very much.' Joe, the other agent, moved over to give him a seat.

"'Where are you headed?' I asked. 'I'm on my way back to Las Vegas,' he replied. 'Started out early this morning hitchhiking for Los Angeles, but I decided to turn back. Been walking since noon. Nobody stopped for me till you.'

"There was something odd about him. To the eye he looked like one of thousands of homeless derelicts, but to the ear he sounded like a man of breeding and education. *Strange*, I thought.

"No one spoke much after that. The old man soon fell asleep. Wanda sulked in her seat. Then a roadside restaurant came into view, and I proposed that we stop for lunch. We were overdue for it. The others agreed, so I pulled off the road and parked in front of the building. Before getting out, I turned to the old man, who was now awake, and asked, 'Will you join us, sir?'

"'Must you?' I heard Wanda mutter under her breath.

"'He's probably hungry, just like we are,' I insisted. 'How about it?'

"'No, thank you,' he murmured in a sad, weak voice. 'But I would like to use the men's room.' With that, he opened his door and, with surprising agility, exited. He had gone ahead of us by half a dozen steps and then looked back at us. 'You won't leave me here?' he asked. 'Promise?'

"'I promise,' I assured him. 'We'll all leave together.'

"We finished lunch quickly, Wanda consulting her watch frequently. The old man stayed in the men's room the whole time.

"'Look, it's getting late. Let's get out of here,' Wanda said impatiently.

"'But I promised to wait for the old guy. I wonder what's keeping him?'

"'That's not really our problem, is it? Let's just get out of here.' She rose and made a move for the door.

"'Something must have happened to him. I'd better check,' I said. I walked toward the rest rooms in the rear of the restaurant. At that moment the old man reappeared.

"'Thanks for waiting for me,' he murmured. "I felt a little sick. A touch of sunstroke, maybe. I'm okay now. Thanks for waiting.'

"'No problem,' I said. But we are running a little late.'

"The old man looked me dead in the eye. 'Are you in real estate?' he asked pleasantly.

"'Yes. How did you know?'

"'I heard you talking. I know a little about real estate. May I have your card?'

"Dubiously, but because he asked for it, I gave him one. He put it in his tattered jacket without looking at it.

"'I appreciate your kindness,' he whispered. 'I'll send you a little token of thanks.'

"'It's not necessary,' I said. 'Glad to be of help. Are you ready to go? Sure you won't have a quick sandwich or something to go?'

"'No. And I'll manage nicely from here. I appreciate the ride.'

"'You're welcome to come to Las Vegas. It's another 50 miles,' I said to him.

"'No. I'll manage from here,' he said quietly. He thrust out a bony hand, conspicuous with its long fingernails, and I shook it gently. Then, fixing me once more with his black, steady eyes, he said, as though sharing a great secret, 'There's great wealth out there. Uranium. Remember that.'

"I assured him I would and left the restaurant.

"Wanda, Joe, and I reached the ranch property, inspected it in the late afternoon light, and then turned around and drove home, hardly exchanging a word. By the end of the trip I had decided to quit Wanda's firm. I didn't see any real future working with her. For her part, I'm sure she had no use for idlers who wasted time picking up tramps on the highway. I began looking for a new job at once."

"So you came here?" asked Paula.

"I'm not quite finished with the story," Claudia said with a smile.

"Go on, please," invited Paula.

Exactly a week later I received a large registered envelope postmarked in Las Vegas. 'Who do I know in Las Vegas?' I asked myself. I brought it with me today. Would you care to look at it, Ms. Rem?"

Claudia pulled out a large white envelope from her attaché case, extracted its contents, and handed them to Paula.

"Looks like a deed, and a letter," Paula said. "The letter is addressed to you. It says, 'Dear Ms. Adams: You kept your promise to me and I am keeping my promise to send you a little token of my appreciation.'"

Paula paused, then suddenly exclaimed, "It's signed, 'Howard Hughes'!"

"It's him all right," said Claudia. "He sent me a gift of one thousand acres of desert property. Bona fide. I'm the legal owner of it. I've been to the registry."

"Some little token of appreciation!" said Paula.

"The way I figure it, it was for picking him up and then keeping my promise to wait for him in that restaurant," added Claudia. "Now you know why I came in here for a job: it was the slogan under your company name."

Paula looked across her desk into the face of the woman she had only just met. She thought for a moment and then said, smiling, "Forget the references and the application. You've got a job with Rem Realty as of now." She reached out her hand.

Claudia shook it firmly. "When do I start?" she asked, her eye on a vacant desk nearby.

◆ ◆ ◆ ◆

C laudia didn't truck very long with people who treat promises to "useless" people with contempt. She had her eye out for an employer she could work *with*, rather than *for*. And so she moved on as soon as she could to greener pastures, those being the ones fertilized and watered by goodwill. She was attracted to a job where making and keeping promises to others was the *modus operandi*, the method of procedure. She and Paula will get along fine. They will each sell a lot of houses and have fun doing it.

3

—

DEFINING
GOODWILL

—

I n line with the oft-quoted saying, "When the pupil is
ready, the teacher appears," our third soap opera takes us
to a workshop on goodwill in which a group of salespeople learns something crucial, although belatedly. What was it
that helped these people get ready to learn it? Could it have
been other than the persuasiveness of a great yet simple truth
that all had somehow missed? And, as a result, had they been
kept from real success in their careers? It is never too late to
learn; indeed, the very persuasiveness of a truth is sharpest
for those who have suffered from trying to succeed on half-
truths and downright falsehoods.

✦✦✦✦

W anda Armstrong, the real estate broker we met in the
previous chapter, sat in the third row of the classroom,
facing the lecturer. She had spent $300 to attend a series of
workshops for brokers called "Successful Real Estate
Selling" and was only half-listening to the lecture. The topic

was "Creating Goodwill." Wanda had really wanted to be in another class, a workshop entitled "How to Close," which was being held simultaneously, but it was full. So, reluctantly, she came to this one. Creating goodwill, indeed! She already *knew* what created goodwill—any idiot knew. She just couldn't imagine a three-hour workshop on the subject. But, rather than lose one-fifth of her money, she had decided to attend anyway and sat there now, resigned to her fate for the next three hours. And, if she needed confirmation of her agony, she felt she had it in the lecturer who stood before her, a tall, rumpled, bearded type who was sure to be long on theory and short on nitty-gritty. Right now the man was busy trying to get responses from the class on what goodwill really was. There was no shortage of hands, and Wanda, to relieve her boredom more than anything else, had raised her hand. The lecturer acknowledged her and invited her to comment.

Wanda didn't hesitate. "Goodwill is something you create in people by being friendly to them, smiling, showing interest."

"I see," the lecturer said. "Somebody else, perhaps with another view of it?"

The man sitting in front of Wanda disagreed. "Goodwill is something you create by doing your customers favors. Like telling then about special discounts, ways to save money, things like that," he insisted.

"Somebody else with another idea?" inquired the lecturer.

A rather stout man in the rear immediately boomed out, "Goodwill is a kind of credit accumulated after years in business by serving customers well. It's an asset, something that adds to the value of a business."

"Only to a *business?* How about to the individual? Doesn't he or she accumulate goodwill as well?" asked the lecturer in three rapid-fire questions to his audience of some 30 men and women.

Wanda listened to the parrying with increasing distaste. Just make-work, she thought. There's no content, so the guy just stalls, shooting the breeze with everybody. She looked around. No one seemed to be aware of the big shuck going on. *People are sheep, that's all. No hope for them,* she thought. Sixty bucks! That's what I'm throwing away on this lemon. Sixty bucks to prove that water is wet. When will I stop being a sucker for every "expert" who comes down the pike, offering "knowledge" for a fat fee?

"Can anybody give a concrete example of the creation of goodwill?" the lecturer asked.

Wanda could. She was tempted to tell the story of a former member of her staff, Claudia Adams, who had befriended a tramp in the desert one day and was rewarded with a deed to some property the "tramp" owned. God, what luck! And then, after Wanda had made it all possible, the worker had walked out on her. *You'd think she could have shared a little of her good fortune,* Wanda thought angrily, *given me, say, 10 percent of her take.* It was all too painful to think about. One thing it taught her, though: friendliness pays. *No,* she thought, *she wouldn't tell that story.* No one would believe it, and she would rather forget the whole incident.

The lecturer went on. "Look, you people are in the selling

business. You know how important goodwill is. But do you really know *what* it is? How is it created? So far I haven't heard anybody who has a clear idea of it or even comes close to it."

A voice piped up. "Charm. Personality. That's how you create goodwill. Smile a lot. Get your customers to like you. When you do that, they buy." This came from a very attractive blonde sitting in the front row and brought a hoot from several of the men.

"You've got what it takes. How about when you're bald and 50?" shouted a bald 50-year-old man at the end of the same row.

"And have dandruff and halitosis?" added another voice from the rear.

"And have body odor, too!" sang out another.

The scene was now one of laughter and frivolity. The lecturer joined in the fun for a few moments and then said, "Goodwill is created by making and keeping promises."

There was a profound silence in the room, as though some great revelation had occurred. The lecturer waited, his eyes roving the room for any disagreement. He expected none. Indeed, it was always the same, conference after conference. He was always amazed that such an important truth, with its immense implications and applications, went largely unrecognized among selling professionals. He knew that the silence was a pregnant one in which the minds of his listeners were filled with instant replays of their various selling successes and failures. Their staring faces were saying to him,

"So that's why I'm not further along in this business than I might be!"

"Any questions?" the lecturer asked with a smile.

◆◆◆◆

Why did the explanation of goodwill command such respectful silence? Because its obviousness was at once breathtaking and humbling. Then, too, there were the immediate, interior consultations of past memories for why this sale or that sale didn't get off the ground. "Any questions?" the instructor had asked. Perhaps later there would be a few, but at that moment there was a stillness in the workshop audience. Wanda Armstrong, for one, was busy remembering what happened that day in the desert, when a certain "derelict" materialized on the highway to Las Vegas.

4

—

CREATING GOODWILL

—

G iven the crucial importance of goodwill to success in the selling field, it is incredible how much uncertainty—indeed, downright mystery—abounds about its creation.

This cannot be because of a complexity that renders it accessible only to the minds of rocket scientists. Creating goodwill is as simple as ABC. Nor can this uncertainty be because of any lack of interest on the part of salespeople, who are forever flirting with the subject.

How then to account for it?

One answer may be found in the peculiar "hiddenness" of things that are taken for granted.

Goodwill is like the air we breathe, the service rendered at a first-class hotel, the availability of energy to light the road at night, or the strength it takes to simply scratch one's nose. It is often taken for granted and goes unnoticed—until it is absent.

"I wonder why the welcome mat is no longer out for me?" Joe Salesman asks.

Simple. You made a promise to a client you didn't keep.

"Nobody's perfect," Joe insists. "I often say things I don't really mean. Everybody does. It's called The Game of Friendly Banter."

The client heard you promise delivery on Monday.

"I told him what he wanted to hear, not what I seriously intended to do for him," Joe replies.

That's why the welcome mat got yanked. You made a promise you didn't keep.

"They're being babies," says Joe scornfully. "Babies cry when they don't get their bottle on time."

Yanking the welcome mat is the adult equivalent of a baby's crying. Both are forms of nonverbal communication. The message goes to the very heart of all human relations: break your promise to me and I complain, as loudly as necessary. The client is not being a baby; he's being genuinely and unalterably human.

"You've got my attention. Tell me more."

Promise to listen?

"I promise."

How can I be sure you mean it? That you're not engaging in—what did you call it?—The Game of Friendly Banter?

"Trust me. This time I mean what I say."

I'd like to, but your betrayal of the client affects my welcome mat as well.

"Why? I haven't broken any promise to you."

True, but why do I deserve any better treatment than your customer got?

"I get your point. I've been treating some people better than others."

And anybody who learns this about you is bound to wonder if it is his or her turn to be lied to.

"Lied to? That's rather strong."

Strong enough to make people who know about your treatment of some of your customers wary of you.

"Then I was foolish to tell you about my problem."

The foolish part was making an idle promise. It cost you the thing you need to succeed as a salesperson, namely, your customer's goodwill.

"It's a small account. Losing it won't cripple me."

No, but losing anyone's goodwill is no small matter. It can ruin your day. And it should.

"Why? It's only one account, one person."

Because everything in this world is connected. Take a smooth pond of water, for example. What happens when you drop a small pebble into the center of it?

"You get ripples."

Exactly. And before long the whole surface is affected. Remember what wise old Uncle Remus once said: "You kin hide the fire, but what you gonna do with the smoke?"

"Keep talking. This grabs me."

Lying sends out smoke signals.

"How?"

For one thing, people smell the smoke on your clothes.

"How do you mean that?"

Let me give you an instant replay—something we will

look at more closely in a later chapter. Your next customer walks into your office and smells the smoke. He says, "What's the matter? Get up on the wrong side of the bed this morning?" You say, "I was feeling great until a customer got nasty with me." Are you now going to confess to this man what you did to make this customer get nasty? In all honesty, would you say to him, "Well, I promised delivery on Monday, but I was lying to him. I was playing The Game of Friendly Banter?"

"Of course not. Do you think I'm stupid?"

How smart is it to play The Game of Friendly Banter with anyone?

"It's real dumb. I see that now."

Do you see that creating goodwill comes from making and keeping promises, and doing so unfailingly with *all* your customers?

"Yes. I do now. I didn't before, though."

Do you understand that everything and everybody are connected; that you cannot segregate your actions or your customers at whim; that the "smoke" of creating bad will attaches to your clothing, affects your mind and spirit and demoralizes you? The first effect is the loss of respect for yourself; the second is for customers to lose respect for you and withdraw their welcome mat. No one wants to do business with a liar. Each of us absolutely depends on getting the correct information. Falsehoods can be costly and even fatal. And remember, there are no "little lies." With each one you tell, your nose grows longer, as Pinocchio found out, and the weight of it pulls you down.

"Question. How can I win back that customer's goodwill?"

By telling him the truth. That you were playing the Game of Friendly Banter with him. That you are sorry and won't ever do it again. And ask him if he would give you another chance to prove that whatever you promise to do for him will be a promise you mean and you intend to keep.

"Will that do it?"

It will, provided you always remember that trust is earned by worthy behavior done unfailingly each day with everyone you meet.

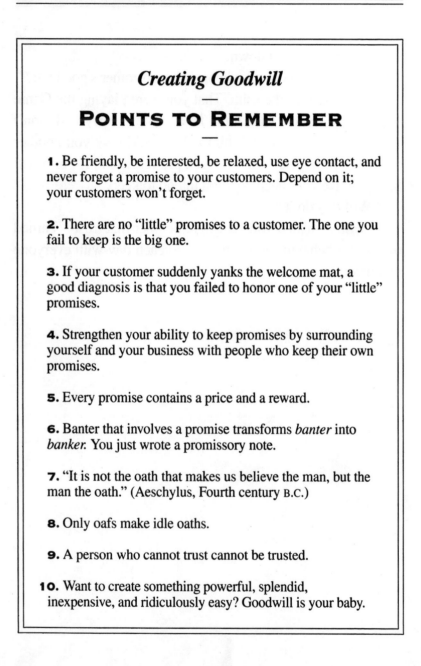

Creating Goodwill

—

POINTS TO REMEMBER

—

1. Be friendly, be interested, be relaxed, use eye contact, and never forget a promise to your customers. Depend on it; your customers won't forget.

2. There are no "little" promises to a customer. The one you fail to keep is the big one.

3. If your customer suddenly yanks the welcome mat, a good diagnosis is that you failed to honor one of your "little" promises.

4. Strengthen your ability to keep promises by surrounding yourself and your business with people who keep their own promises.

5. Every promise contains a price and a reward.

6. Banter that involves a promise transforms *banter* into *banker.* You just wrote a promissory note.

7. "It is not the oath that makes us believe the man, but the man the oath." (Aeschylus, Fourth century B.C.)

8. Only oafs make idle oaths.

9. A person who cannot trust cannot be trusted.

10. Want to create something powerful, splendid, inexpensive, and ridiculously easy? Goodwill is your baby.

II

—

SELF-MANAGEMENT

—

Just say to yourself what you would be;
then do what you have to do.

—Epictetus, Greek philosopher

5

—

CATCHING UP AFTER FALLING BEHIND

—

I t was late at night, after the family had retired, and he sat alone, poring over the bills scattered on his desk. "What's the matter with me, anyway?" he asked himself. "That Rose policy. I should have gotten the renewal. He was my client. I meant to get around to converting his policies over from term, but I delayed getting to it. Then without warning, he goes to Mutual Insurance." He pushed his fingers through his thick head of hair, which was turning gray at the temples.

"Too much time with Little League and TV in the evening," he muttered. "Too often putting things off until tomorrow. I come home with a mountain of work, have the best of intentions to get to it, and then comes dinner, a romp with the kids, a bit of TV, and it's time to go to bed. *Time.* I don't seem to have enough of it. Where does it go? Gotta get organized, work out a time budget, get rough on people who want to small-talk over the phone for an hour. Get rough on myself. Say no and mean it. There's not enough money coming in. I have to put in more hours, work at night. Then there are all the innovations in the field: new computer programs, new rules, new laws. I'm swamped. I'll go back to school and take some courses. I'm losing business because I don't know the answers to an awful lot of questions. Clients sense it. I'm faking it half the time. I make a promise to look up the answer, but I don't. I put it off, forget about it. I'm in big trouble. I'm not competing. This is a rough business. The soft ones get swept away. Gotta toughen up. Do the things I mean to do. Take myself in hand."

✦✦✦✦

We have been listening to the self-talk of a salesman who has many good intentions, or pseudo-promises, to do what he ought to do in his business. Sadly, these intentions are never real or deep enough to prevail over his bodily inclinations. What he *means* to do and what he actually *does* to make a go of selling insurance are somehow always different. He doesn't make his intentions "stick"; there is always something else, usually something praiseworthy in itself, such as spending time with his family, which commands his attention and preempts his time.

Predictably, he has fallen behind. It worries him deeply, but he doesn't know precisely how to solve his problem. He envies people who have the self-discipline to do their homework, and he wishes he had more will power to turn his intentions into earnings. He thinks he is missing some key element of character.

He is missing something, of course, but it has nothing to do with character. It has everything to do with *meaning* his intentions. He has been kidding himself, although he isn't fully aware of it.

◆ ◆ ◆ ◆

L et us now bring our story a little closer to home. I am feeling lazy after a satisfying dinner, watching my favorite sitcom and ignoring some pressing paperwork I brought home.

How do I get myself up and over to my desk?

There is one absolutely dependable way, and that is to promise myself to get up when the show ends, and then simply to keep my promise.

Will such a strategy *absolutely* get me to work? Yes. *How* does it get me to work?

Here comes the key part and the crucial intuition: I get out of my chair and go to work *because I promised myself to do so*. That is the reason. And it is not because I fear unpreparedness on the job, or any other mundane reason. The creation of goodwill is as essential in the society of myself as it is in the larger society.

Promises made to myself must be kept. I cannot get away with lying to myself, even in "little matters."

In self-promising, perhaps even more than in social-promising, there are no "little matters." Any broken self-promise wounds me in my self-respect, and any loss of self-respect weakens a link in the chain connecting me to my will to live and to thrive. Lying to myself—let us not mince words—means cutting away the ground on which I stand. It is a self-betrayal with profoundly serious consequences.

I mean, if I don't attend to that "little matter" *now,* having promised myself to do so, what promise will I dependably keep? How can I depend upon myself to keep a future promise if I won't keep the one I just made? Perhaps I didn't really *mean* to keep it in the first place. Okay, then, what will it take to make a promise I intend to keep? What will it take to motivate me?

I am very motivated by the perception of imminent danger to myself and to my loved ones. I have a binding promise already in place to rescue my family if my house is on fire. I would be out of my easy chair in a flash. That kind of promise to myself I *know* I will keep.

But isn't breaking a promise to myself to get out of my easy chair and tackle the backlog of work dangerous? Yes, it is! Breaking such a promise got Joe Salesman into his fix in chapter 4, and things are going to get worse very soon unless he mends his ways. What ways are those? They are, simply, breaking promises to himself.

If I don't mean to keep the self-promise I make, I had better not make it. Why? Because breaking a promise will compromise my *next* promise. Break two in a row, and the self-promise to keep the third is up for grabs.

Break that one, and I will hear these words echoing in my consciousness: "I can't trust myself anymore to do the things

I promise myself to do!"

Breaking *any* promise, large or little, is dangerous to life and limb.

If a person cannot depend on himself or herself to keep a promise, then indeed, when that person makes the very next one, he or she will be seriously in need of rescue. The next chapter focuses on how to save oneself from the ultimate betrayal—that of one's own self.

6

—

THE
DANGER OF
SELF-BETRAYAL

—

C ornelia was a compulsive worker. She was president of an insurance company, married, and on her way to becoming a millionaire before she was 35. She had promised herself, solemnly, that on the day her accountant told her she had assets of $1 million, she would immediately book first-class passage for two on a cruise ship—to Alaska if it was summer, to the Caribbean if it was winter. That day came sooner than she expected.

Cornelia had been working on a very large, complicated policy for the head of a steel company. The phone chirped in her office. It was Fred, her accountant.

"Hi, Fred. What's up?"

"Just calling to say that the commission from the Harvey policy carried you into the charmed circle. You are now officially a millionaire. Congratulations."

"Hey, that's great news for a worker in the salt mines! I'm thrilled. I couldn't have done it without your investment help,

Fred. I can never thank you enough."

"That's good of you to say. Well, just wanted to let you know."

Cornelia put down the phone. She was both thrilled and troubled by the call. She remembered her solemn promise to herself, made a year earlier but still fresh in her mind, to call the travel agency the same day she got the news. She leaned back in her comfortable swivel chair and thought about it. She had meant it. It was a kind of deep self-contract, a reward to herself for years of hard work. It was to be a reminder that she was something more than a breadwinner, a slave to her insecurities, a drone. She would turn away from her compulsion, her need to prove herself. She and Brad would have two carefree weeks away from everything. It was to be her declaration of freedom from the nitty-gritty of life.

A million dollars. Cornelia thought about it. "Was it enough?" she asked herself. "Am I really out of the woods? Is now the time to relax? How much is a dollar worth nowadays? Prices are out of sight. Mortgage payments, taxes, insurance..." Her face darkened. She thought about her widowed mother in Vermont, about her youngest brother, recovering from a near-fatal auto accident, about her and Brad's plans to start a family. Her husband's income prospects were limited: he was a free-lance writer with one soon-to-be-published first novel under his belt.

"No," she said. "A million dollars is not enough. Two million dollars should have been my target. Then I'd really have some breathing room." She thought of her promise to book have some breathing room." She thought of her promise to book the cruise the same day she got the word. "No. It was a rash promise. Unrealistic." She would put it out of her mind. Impractical. Visionary. She would do it when she hit *two* million. Promise.

She went back to work, congratulating herself that she had not told Brad or anyone else about the promise and the cruise, not even her accountant. Her promise was safe with her. She could break it with impunity.

That evening, on her way home from work, Cornelia had her first drink in nine years. She didn't know why. It just suddenly seemed not to matter anymore that she had been sober all these years. She felt cheated by life. Where were all the glittering prizes, the gongs announcing that she had made it? She had become a millionaire, something that she had always dreamed of becoming. But she felt not one bit different. The world was the same as before, and she was the same as before—no healthier, no more attractive, no wiser. She was a millionaire? Why, she couldn't even afford a 14-day cruise. What kind of millionaire was that?

Cornelia got good and drunk that night. Later she woke up in a midtown hotel with no idea how she got there. Her first thought was to get another drink. Her second was to call Brad—but not until she had a corking good "eye opener" delivered promptly to her room.

She never managed to call Brad, who arrived at the hotel in mid-afternoon. He had been up all night, certain that something terrible had happened to his wife, and had finally tracked her down by calling every hotel in town.

It took Brad a lot of pounding on the door and pleading to get Cornelia to open the door. "Go 'way," she kept saying. "I'm just a broken-down millionaire. Jus' go 'way."

Finally, she stumbled to the door, turned the deadbolt, and flung open the door. "Hello, Brad," she said, and then flopped back onto the unmade bed, burying her head under the pillow.

Brad closed the door behind him and sat down in an armchair, his eyes red and puffy from having been up all night. "We've got to get you home, Cornelia," he said tactfully.

Cornelia agreed, subject to his buying her a bottle on the way home.

Within an hour she was in her own bed, fast asleep. She had finished off half the bottle of whiskey that Brad had reluctantly bought on the way. Sighing, Brad crawled in next to her and soon fell asleep.

When Cornelia woke up, it was early evening, and her brother-in-law, Bob, was sitting in the bedroom. Brad was standing next to the bed. He had awakened an hour earlier and asked his brother, a physician, to stop by. "Hi, Bob," Cornelia said, sitting up. Then she groaned and flopped back onto the pillow, her hands cradling her head. "Oh, I've got a whopping headache."

"You've had a lot to drink, Cornelia," observed the physician in a mildly reproving voice. "Why, Cornelia? Why did you start again when everything was going so well?"

"I don't know, Bob. I suddenly felt it wasn't worth the struggle anymore. I needed to block out the world, I guess."

struggle anymore. I needed to block out the world, I guess."

"Something must have happened, Cornelia. Try to remember."

"I can't. Got a splitting headache."

"Aspirin will fix that." Bob went into the bathroom for some water. "Here, take these," he ordered, handing Cornelia several white pills.

"Will these help a weakling recover her moral strength?" asked the still-prone figure.

"I don't think so. They're just aspirin."

"What will it take, Bob?"

"You have weaknesses like all of us do, Cornelia, but you have demonstrated plenty of moral fiber in the last nine years. Look at this house. You worked to get it, didn't you? You were sober for a long nine years. All right, you took a drink last night. So what? That's not the end of the world. Just get up and make another promise. You'll have another nine or even 59 years of sobriety."

Cornelia put the pills in her mouth and drained the water glass. "God, what a night. I just started to drink and kept going. I don't remember a thing after the fifth drink. Some kind soul must have registered me in that hotel." Then she suddenly remembered something. "My wallet! I had money, credit cards, license, everything in it!"

"Brad has it. That kind soul didn't rip you off. You were lucky."

"Thank goodness," she murmured. Then, suddenly, her eyes lit up. "I think I know what happened to me yesterday. I may be wrong, but I think I know."

Brad was pacing the room. "Care to tell us?" he asked.

"Sure. It has to do with breaking promises to myself. I want to see if I'm right. Hand me the Yellow Pages, will you, Brad darling?"

Mystified, Brad dug the book out of a bottom drawer and handed it to her. Cornelia flipped through the pages for a few seconds and then reached for the phone. "I think, just possibly, I'm going to be all right," she said as she dialed a certain number. "I think I'll be able to get back on track," she said cryptically.

◆◆◆◆

Cornelia had been relaxing in a deck chair for almost an hour. The sun was warm and she lay there, dreamy and comfortable. The chimes rang for lunch, and the sound brought her back to the reality of the first day of a 14-day Caribbean cruise. She turned to Brad, seated restfully in the chair next to her, and smiled. "Hungry, darling?" she asked. "Let's see what the chef has prepared for two happy people who have more than earned a trip on a slow boat to paradise."

◆◆◆◆

Cornelia was able to pull herself out of a very serious tailspin because she suddenly realized the importance of her self-promise. Although not all broken self-promises have such dramatic consequences, don't dismiss this breach of self-contract as a trivial thing.

7

—

THE PROMISE
LAND

—

T he most basic and important society is the society of
yourself.

Although we tend to think of society as involving
more than one person, language affirms the reality of the self-
society. Thus we have the phrase "Be good to yourself," or,
"Take a good look at yourself."

The basic law of self-society is this: *You must not lie to
yourself.* If you do so, dire consequences are inescapable.

No matter what the "advantage" a lie to yourself may
confer, you pay a price for it, and sometimes it's frightfully
high.

Self-promising is serious business. The loss of self-credibility is no minor matter. You continually need to be able to
count on yourself to do (or to avoid) the things that will sus-
tain growth (or incur disaster).

Therefore, do not make promises to yourself idly or rashly.

A self-promise must be prudent, taking realistically into
account your strengths and weaknesses as time has revealed
them. Thus, you do not promise yourself to do anything

unless you *mean* to do it, which implies that you must perceive first of all that you *can*.

Take the Delphic oracle's temple inscription "Know thyself," to heart.

Self-promises are an important way to get things done, a way of gaining control over future events by deploying your reserves of time and energy to that future.

The words *I promise* (whether to yourself or to another) may be said to create the future, endowing it with significance and relieving it of its awful uncertainty.

It is playing God with time. Only God is said to know the future, yet the person who *knows* he or she will deliver on a promise—whether it is to oneself or to another—has a kind of glimpse into the future.

Making and keeping a promise is a powerful delivery system of human energy. It is a mechanism for helping and extending human possibility, a device for creating opportunity and, perhaps above all, for displaying and testing moral fiber, whether it is you own or that of another. This by no means exhausts the list of what "promising" is in human affairs.

Promising—whether it be to yourself or to another—combines curiosity (will you or the other person keep the promise?), excitement (if the other person keeps her promise, how thrilling it will be! If not, how awful, how revealing of her!), doubt, dread, and other mental states as well.

The self-promise is not idle. It is a hard calculation of your true power projected over future time. It is a draft of future time, a rational attempt to control it and make it "pay its way" toward your success and happiness.

Yet having said this, and for all the seriousness of the self-promise, a breach of it, singly or even continuously over a long period of time, need not be an irreversible calamity.

The remedy for the inevitable loss of self-credibility that follows from breaking a self-promise is to make the promise anew, this time more earnestly, more genuinely, more solemnly.

You can *learn* to keep your promises, as you learn to do other things. The next time you are offered an uncontaminated "place" to take a fresh stand—that is, to make a new promise with a new intention to keep it—seize the opportunity and make good on your promise. Time will reveal whether you really mean what you promise yourself, and how sincere and authentic you are.

And, most important of all, time will reveal whether you can plan your future and count on the future you plan.

Self-promising is a pivotal strategy. It is the road to the land that you have promised yourself to reach.

It is the way to travel hopefully and to arrive with your hopes intact.

The Law of Self-Promise is this: I will not distrust myself until I break my promise to self; I will not trust myself again until I begin faithfully to keep it.

Who but the dreamer would want it any other way?

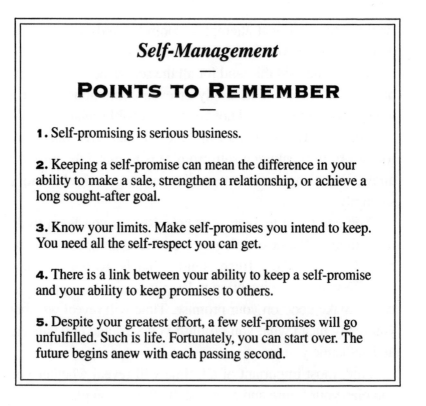

Self-Management

—

POINTS TO REMEMBER

—

1. Self-promising is serious business.

2. Keeping a self-promise can mean the difference in your ability to make a sale, strengthen a relationship, or achieve a long sought-after goal.

3. Know your limits. Make self-promises you intend to keep. You need all the self-respect you can get.

4. There is a link between your ability to keep a self-promise and your ability to keep promises to others.

5. Despite your greatest effort, a few self-promises will go unfulfilled. Such is life. Fortunately, you can start over. The future begins anew with each passing second.

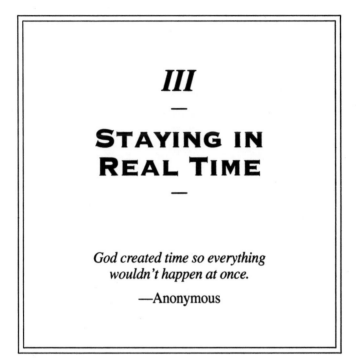

III

—

STAYING IN
REAL TIME

—

*God created time so everything
wouldn't happen at once.*

—Anonymous

8

—

TIME ON YOUR HANDS

—

It cannot be said too often: Time is to be lived, not to be thought. If I think, *How am I going to put up with another day of unproductive leads?* I am thinking time, not living it. Such "time" is imaginary, which is to say *unreal.* Such "time" bears as much relation to real time as the thought of a cold drink on a sweltering summer day bears to the reality of the actual drink cascading down my parched throat.

Thinking time.

Correction: Thinking "time." For real time cannot be *thought* into existence. Real time is now and only now.

Imaginary "time," however, can be thought. Such "time" comes into existence only when I think it and only in real time or now time.

This means I cannot think *about* imaginary "time." Such "time" does not come before my act of thinking. It is not "out there," as it were, waiting to be thought about.

The word *about* is a mischief maker. When I say, "I am going to think *about* my problem," the word *about* implies that the problem is there, large and looming, independent of my act of thinking. In fact, it is not.

The mischief comes from confusing two completely distinct states of reality, namely the state of being a thing and the state of being a thought.

Such confusion can lead to serious consequences.

This brings us to another series of soap operas. In this chapter and the two that follow, a day in the lives of three salesmen unfolds. Each salesman is intelligent and therefore capable of finding success and fulfillment in his work. Intelligence proves not to be the decisive factor, however, in the living-out of his day.

What is decisive is *how each uses real time.*

We will see how one salesman begins the day thinking "time" into existence rather than living it each moment. Such "time" quickly demoralizes him. His day goes from bad to worse as he continues to think "time" rather than to live it.

The second salesman lives a kind of amphibious life, like a seal, sometimes in the "water" of imaginary "time," at other times on the "dry land" of real time.

Finally, we will see that the third salesman is a real-time person. We will follow him from the moment he wakes— early and raring to go—to his day at his auto dealership.

Again, none of these men is more intelligent, more eager to succeed, than the other.

Each is capable of having a flourishing sales career.

And each, even the salesman whom we call the "real-time person," can benefit from a full realization that real time is now and is to be lived, not thought.

Each, therefore, would benefit from reading Part Four of this book, which is entitled "Self-Understanding."

Let us now take a look at our next set of soap operas.

◆◆◆◆

B en reached for the ringing alarm clock and shut it off. He was awake. Another day had begun for him.

He didn't feel like getting out of bed. This was the third day of his new job, and he thought about how much he hated it.

Outside his bedroom window the sun shone brightly and birds chirped away, drowned out now and then by the roaring engine of an occasional passing car. Not that Ben noticed; he was already thinking how bad and wearying life was.

Minutes went by as he lay there in bed, thinking. He visualized the car showroom where he worked, his little desk in a cubicle, the telephone resting on top, daring him to use it, mocking him.

"Make 12 telephone calls every day and you'll make money." That was easy enough for Bill Johnson, the manager of the dealership, to say—he didn't have to face the rejections and the rudeness. People were just plain mean. That was it in a nutshell. Either they didn't want a new car or had relatives in the car business. Either that or they didn't really need a car. How was he expected to find the needle in the haystack, the person who was just waiting with a down payment, excellent credit, and a trade-in?

"Keep making the calls." That's all he ever heard.

Ben lay in bed for another half hour, thinking. He didn't see the point to getting up. Finally his hunger overcame his inertia and he got up. He showered, barely feeling the strong spray of water on his body until it suddenly ran hot. Then he quickly ducked out from under the water and cursed loudly. Someone in the apartment above or below him had flushed the toilet.

Ben dried himself, working a towel across his back, catching the little globules of water that clung here and there to his body. He was scarcely aware of the towel, however. This morning he had chosen, as usual, to produce in his mind a variety of gloomy thoughts about work: endless, unproductive phone calls, canceled orders, window-shoppers, and so forth, which brought him close to going back to bed—and probably losing his job. Bed and sleep at least offered him relief from his unperceived self-wounding.

Ben sat at the breakfast table in his bathrobe for a half hour. He was on his fifth cup of coffee. Occasionally he got up and went to the stove or the refrigerator for something, then came back to his chair. To all appearances he was having his breakfast, but in fact he hardly noticed his food—he was lost in thought during the whole meal.

He glanced at the clock on the wall. It was time to get dressed and go to work. He sighed, got up, put on his clothes, and went to the door of his small apartment.

A five-minute drive brought him to the automobile dealership where he worked. He parked his car in the usual spot, and in a minute he was through the front door and on his way to his desk.

◆◆◆◆

Clearly, Ben has been thinking "time" rather than living it. As a result his day was, in a real sense, already "old" when he arrived for work. What he needed was a fresh start for the day; instead, he dosed himself with so many unbearable thoughts that he was "out of it" by the time he got to work.

Had he gotten out of the imaginary "time" of his thoughts and into the real time of his work, he could have had a good day.

Ben had stopped being his own contemporary. He had successfully put himself out of sync with the opportunities of his job by "mugging" himself. He was busy pouring his precious time down the sink of his mind.

Ben did not see that there is nothing more vital to a healthy, successful life than an understanding and use of real time.

◆◆◆◆

Before we go on to the next salesman's day, a few additional remarks about time are in order.

Real time seems simple enough, but when you think

about it, it takes on an awesome complexity.

St. Augustine, who got off to a slow start in life, said this about time: "When I don't think about it, I know what it is; when I think about it, then I don't know what it is."

The problem of time comes from the fact that we humans can imagine time. We can visualize yesterday and tomorrow. What's more, we can visualize ourselves in some yesterday or tomorrow so vividly that we might be said to be there—almost, but not quite.

There is simply no way to be in visualized or imaginary time. For better or for worse, as long as we have bodies, each of us is anchored firmly and inescapably in real time.

What is real time?

Real time is now. There is perhaps no more accurate way to put it. *NOW*. We were conceived, born, had our first meal, took every breath we have ever taken *in a now*.

You have doubts?

Let us suppose you are determined to escape the now, to do something outside of it. Will you be successful? No.

Let us say you want to wink your eye, an easy enough operation, surely. Try, if you can, to do it yesterday. Try to do it even a second ago. Did you succeed? In fact, you *thought* of yesterday and then imagined yourself winking in it. Did you have a vivid picture of yourself winking yesterday? Okay, but when did you actually do the imagining? Wasn't it actually in a definite now?

Our little exercise with winking clearly shows two facts: (1) that all events, including imaginary ones, happen in a *now,* and (2) that yesterday and tomorrow—even a split second from now—are entirely mental states of being.

A closer look at these two facts will reveal some astonishing information about real time, with some very important practical implications.

Real time, the now, comes and goes instantly. Yet it is "long enough," if we may put it that way, for every event of the entire universe to occur in it, ranging from those on the most distant planet to those on earth, whether inside or outside our consciousness.

The importance of the now is made clear by one simple fact of human experience: every event has to wait for a particular now in which to occur and, once it occurs, it slips immediately into the past.

The now may be looked on as a very narrow "corridor" of time in which every physical or physically based event, such as an act of the human memory or imagination, occurs. Such events, always occurring in now time, can be called "temporal" events.

Real time is now. It is not a creation of human thought.

Time is to be lived, not to be thought.

Let us move on to the day of another salesman, the one who lives amphibiously, like a seal, in real time and in imaginary "time."

9

—

THE TIME IMPERATIVE

—

W itness a day in the life of Hiram Hynes, car sales- man. Selling cars has been his whole working life, and he has settled into it with some degree of success. He has managed to support his family comfortably, but not without a continual struggle. Real time is not as much a working ally as it could be.

◆◆◆◆

H iram lay in bed as he heard his wife calling him. Her voice meant that breakfast, piping hot, was about to go on the table. He tossed the covers aside, heaved himself up, and sat on the edge of the bed, scratching himself. He would have slept all day if his wife hadn't called.

In five seconds he was on his feet. He found his slippers and bathrobe and made it in and out of the bathroom in less than two minutes—just enough time to splash some cold water on his face.

His wife was working at the stove as Hiram entered the

kitchen. She greeted him with a "Good morning, dear."

The Hyneses had twin girls, just finishing high school, who were like Hiram in their reluctance to get a move on in the morning. *Chips off the old block,* he thought.

He kissed his wife on the cheek and lowered his ample bulk into his chair at the table, sniffing the freshly brewed coffee in the percolator. Ah, breakfast! What would the world be without it? What would the world be without Grace and the kids, without the house, without the job?

The job. Until that moment Hiram hadn't thought about the job. Most times he managed to go all the way to the dealership itself without once thinking about the fact that he was a car salesman. But today, for some reason, he did, just as he was about to sip his coffee. It darkened him immediately. No, the job wasn't all that bad. He just didn't like to have to work. If it wasn't for work, he could stay where he now sat as long as he pleased, read the morning paper, loll around the house.

The taste of hot coffee in his mouth brought him back to Grace and the bacon, eggs, and toast laid out on the breakfast plate in front of him. He applied his knife and fork to the task with sheer pleasure. Grace saw the happiness on his face and felt a deep gladness. She smiled at her husband. Hiram was a big boy who, with the right amount of mothering by her, could carry his load very well. Her eye fell on the brand-new refrigerator and stove that Hiram bought as a surprise for her last Christmas, paid for with his end-of-year bonus. She realized how deeply she loved her husband. Right now she was trying to do something about his weight and had buttered his toast very lightly.

"Hey, I can hardly see the butter on this one, Grace," Hiram protested gently. She smiled at him, took back the toast, and added a little more butter—just a little. Hiram liked "cooperation," as he called it, even if it was only a token.

Grace joined her husband at the breakfast table. Hiram leaned over, gave her a big kiss full on the mouth, and looked at her longingly. He suddenly thought he would take the morning off for "other things."

Grace read his thoughts exactly. "Tonight, darling. I promise. You're expecting a customer in 20 minutes, and I want to beat the rush to the market. Otherwise, there'll be nothing left worth eating."

Hiram saw at once the soundness of his wife's logic. He slowly finished his coffee, feeling relaxed as he sat in the cozy kitchen alcove with the yellow curtains and green-flowered wallpaper. Tonight. His mind raced ahead to tonight. But work came first. His face darkened with the thought that he had to go through a whole day at the "sweat factory," as he called it. Then the thought of selling Al Ross that cream-colored four-door sedan cheered him up. He had called Al the day before to tell him about it. Al had said he would come in at eight sharp the next morning to see it. Now Hiram fantasized about his commission check for that week—it would be fat. This would be his third sale of the month. He drained his coffee cup and headed back to the bathroom. In 20 minutes he was ready to leave.

Grace was waiting for him at the door, shopping bag in

hand. They went to the double-car garage, kissed, and got into their separate cars.

He followed his wife out of the driveway, honked good-bye, and drove off down the pleasant, tree-shaded street.

When Hiram arrived at work, Al Ross was already waiting for him. *Damn,* Hiram thought. *I'm late. It was that second cup of coffee.* "Hi, Al. Been waiting long?"

"About 20 minutes," Al replied irritably.

Hiram had goofed and he knew it. Al Ross was a very busy, very successful architect. "Sorry about that," Hiram said. "Let's step into my office."

As soon as he and Al were seated, Hiram proudly pointed to a shiny cream-colored Buick in the showroom. "There's the car I was telling you about, Al. A beauty, isn't she?"

Al looked at the car. "That's not quite the color I had in mind. Too, uh, creamy. Shows the dirt too much. I go through a lot of dusty sites in my work."

After 20 years in the business, Hiram knew an alibi when he heard one. "It's the most popular color in the industry this year," he insisted. "You'll love it. The gas mileage is terrific, and I can give you a great price on it."

"No, I don't think so, Hi," Al said, shaking his head. "It just isn't my car. I think I'll stick with the one I have for one more year." He looked at his watch. "I'm late. I better be getting back to my office. I've got somebody coming by in five minutes."

What could Hiram do? Act graciously. Not show his bitter disappointment over his loss of a "sure thing."

"I'm sorry to see someone else getting the car, Al. It's one of a kind. Don't know when I'll get delivery on another, what with the slowdown and all. Let me show you the inside."

"Thanks, Hi, but not now. I really must be going." The man smiled faintly, rose from his chair, and hurried out the door.

Hiram felt as though he had been hit in the belly. It was the old pain. "All for a lousy 20 minutes," he mumbled. His mind raced, trying to find someone, something to blame. Grace. She had kept him too long at breakfast. No. It was the kids. They can never seem to get their behinds in gear in the morning. "No," Hiram finally said to himself. "It was me. I'm just not organized. Wasting my time in the morning over cups of coffee and idle thoughts about going back to bed with Grace when there is work to be done. Hell! It's nobody's fault but mine. I was late for our appointment. Ross is a stickler for punctuality; he expects everybody to be like him. Can't a fellow be a little late once in a while without it costing him a nice commission?"

Wave after wave of anguish washed over Hiram as he sat in his cubicle. The thought of retiring crossed his mind. He had had enough. People these days are just ridiculous. There are a thousand reasons why a person can be late: accidents, traffic jams...

Hiram punished himself for the better part of half an hour. Then he got up and went to the washroom. He was drying his hands when the door opened and the new salesman, young Ben Davis, walked in.

"How's it going, Ben? Gotten used to the old place yet?" Hiram asked, smiling amiably at his colleague. "It'll take a little while, but you'll fit in and make some money. Keep after it, kid."

Ben forced a smile and murmured, "I'm trying, Hy."

As Hiram left the lavatory, he wondered about Ben. He had seen distress in the young man's face, as if Ben felt he wasn't up to the struggle of selling cars. Hiram remembered himself at age 25, frightened and wet behind the ears, but somehow tougher than the young ones who were coming along these days. He had proved it, too. Twenty-five years in the car business, all at one dealership. And he was far from finished. He had a good 20 years left. The twins will eventually fly the coop—go off and get married—and he and Grace would be together, alone. Retirement? Not for him. Not until he had sold a lot more cars.

He strode back to his office, its walls covered with awards for "Leadership in Sales." Well, it could still be a good week. He settled down to some phone work.

The rejections came thick and fast. Ten of them, one after the other. "Not interested"; "Just bought a car"; "Don't like the current Buicks"; "Saving for my daughter's wedding." All negatives.

Hiram went for coffee. But he came right back and got on the phone to a Mr. Spencer Sill, a cold prospect off the list of new homeowners in town.

"Mr. Sill? I'm Hiram Hynes, down at Paramount Buick. Welcome to town."

"Hello."

"Mr. Sill, I don't know what kind of car you drive, but there are a lot of happy people in town driving Buicks. Like to tell you about our product, if you have a few minutes."

"Well, Mr. Hynes, I do need a new car. And I've owned a Buick or two in my day. How are the prices?"

"Never been better. We're overstocked right now in several models. I can give you a very good buy. Do you have a trade-in, by any chance?"

"I have a five-year-old Chevy that needs a lot of work. It's gotten to the point where I think the wisest thing is to trade it in. Do you take five-year-old Chevys?"

"I'm sure we can work out something satisfactory for you. Could you drive in today and let me look at it?"

"Okay, I'll come right down."

"Good, I'll be waiting. My name is Hiram Hynes."

Bulls-eye, thought Hiram as he hung up the phone. The old statistics, they never fail. Sooner or later, if you keep calling, you hit. He got his contract pad out and did some quick figuring on a five-year-old Chevy. He set a figure below which he wouldn't —couldn't—go on a number of different models. A lot would depend on the Chevy and its condition. If it was a dog, that was one thing; if it had been taken care of, that was another. He found himself humming. The sun had not yet come out from behind the clouds, but the day had definitely become brighter. He went to the coffee machine and drew himself a cup. He came back just in time to see Ben Davis go out the door, get into his car, and drive away. He

wondered what was on the youngster's mind. Too much wor-
rying and not enough working was Hiram's guess. The kind
of stuff he still did a lot of. But he was learning. The kid
would have to learn, too. Or leave the business.

◆◆◆◆

Hiram had missed a sure sale and had only himself to
blame. But he got himself back in the groove, back into
real time, and recovered nicely. Clearly, his grip on real time
was not the best: more hit-and-miss than anything else. The
next chapter is a day in the life of his boss, Bill Johnson.

10

—

TIME WILL
TELL

—

B ill Johnson opened his eyes at exactly 6 A.M. The birds outside his window were, as usual, letting the world know they were around. He sprang out of his warm bed and made his way quietly but quickly to the bathroom. No one else in the family was awake yet. He loved the stillness of the house in the early morning, the feeling of having everything to himself for about an hour. It gave him a jump on things.

His wife stirred as he left the bed. She mumbled something inaudible, and the next moment she was sound asleep again.

After he washed up, Bill went into the kitchen and put water in the percolator for coffee, then went into his "gym" in the family room for his morning exercise. In 15 minutes he had worked up a sweat from vigorous sit-ups and weightlifting. It was a daily ritual, his way of staying in shape. Then he showered, shaved, and did the other necessities before dressing.

It was now almost seven o'clock, and his wife was rousing herself in the bedroom. In a minute or two she appeared in the kitchen in her bathrobe, yawning and rubbing her eyes.

"Morning, Beauty," he said, kissing her.

Mary knew she was hardly beautiful in the morning and wondered if she was ever beautiful anymore, but she appreciated the remark just the same.

"Good morning, Bill," she replied. She dearly loved her husband. What's more, she admired his grip on things and on himself. He was disciplined. She wished she herself had more of it. Living with Bill for 15 years helped, of course. But with her it was mere imitation; Bill had the real thing. Of course, it helped if you went to military school, where you learned early to put your socks away in the right spot.

"Ready for breakfast?" Bill asked. He cooked breakfast every day except Sunday. Mary let him do it, although she had felt guilty at first. Bill liked to do it and he did a good job.

"Kids up yet?" she asked.

"No. I'll go wake them," said Bill, moving quickly away from the stove. He had everything almost ready, and all he needed now was mouths. He opened three bedroom doors and shouted into each room, "Breakfast is now being served. Up and at 'em!"

Each Johnson child knew that he or she wouldn't be called twice, just dumped lovingly but emphatically on the carpeted floor. So they got up almost at once with various groans and complaints. Within five minutes everybody was sitting at the breakfast table in different stages of wakefulness. It was Cecilia's turn to say grace and she did it as if God were still in bed, too.

The conversation turned to the basketball game that night which the whole family was planning to attend. Bill, Jr., the older boy, was the first string center.

"How do the prospects look for tonight, Billy?" asked Bill, Sr.

"We'll take them easy."

"Easily," corrected Mary, a stickler for good speech.

"It won't even be close," piped Jamie, the younger son. "They have a seven-foot center. He'll be eating off Bill's head all night."

"The bigger they come, the harder they fall," said the father.

"I can handle him," Billy said. "I'm faster and smarter."

"Latin won't help much on the rebound," taunted Jamie.

Bill liked positive thinking. Jamie was being negative, however. "Jamie," Bill said, "If Billy says he can handle the big center, who are we to question him? I happen to believe him."

Bill glanced at his watch. He had finished his breakfast and rose from his chair. He looked at Mary and said, "I'm not making any appointments for tonight, dear. Expect me by five o'clock."

"Supper for five at six," said his wife, getting up. "Then the basketball game."

Bill quickly put on his jacket and went to the door. "Let's keep a close eye on Jamie this month," he said to Mary, kissing her good-bye.

Bill backed his big new car out of the garage and onto the

pebble-strewn driveway, glancing back at the English Tudor–style house as he drove off. Years ago he went in over his head to get that house because Mary liked it so much, and he had to scramble for several years to make the payments. "But it was worth it," he told himself again this morning. It had been the perfect house for them and had almost doubled in value in 10 years. He drove out to the street, turned the corner, and in three minutes was on the highway heading for his dealership. *It is so nice to be the boss,* he thought.

It was early fall. The morning was overcast and looked like it would stay cloudy all day. Already the leaves were dropping from the trees. He caught a glimpse of geese flying low against the gray background of the sky; in a second they were gone from his line of sight. Within 10 minutes he was pulling up to Paramount Buick. Yes, it *was* very nice to be the boss. In a few steps Bill was at the front door of his business and putting his key into the lock. *Ten years of hard work gets you the key to the front door,* he thought.

There was a lot of work to do on the computer: tallies to be made of the previous day's business, contracts to be checked, inventories to be taken. Bill settled into his leather chair behind his big desk. He was deep into his morning work when, at the stroke of eight, a customer came in the front door. Bill rose to greet him.

"Good morning. I'm Bill Johnson, the owner of Paramount Buick. Can I help you?"

"I'm Al Ross. I have an appointment with Hiram Hynes. He wants to show me a new Buick."

"I'm sure Hi will be here any second. Must have gotten held up in traffic." Bill saw a wave of annoyance cross the man's face.

"He said he'd be waiting here for me."

"Hiram is usually very punctual. My best salesman. He should be here any second. Can I get you a cup of coffee? Won't you come into my office and make yourself comfortable?"

The man looked at his watch. "No, thank you. I can only wait a few minutes. I have an appointment at 8:30. I'm an architect and I'm understaffed right now."

Bill led the man to a chair in the showroom, hoping the handsome new cars would entertain him for a while. He excused himself and went back into his office. He tried to get back into his work but kept looking for Hiram's car to pull up. Then, just as he was about to call him at home, he saw the familiar burgundy Buick pull into view, 20 minutes late. He saw Hiram greet the man and take him into his own office. Bill crossed his fingers mentally and went back to work. Two minutes later he saw the architect walk out the door. He knew Hiram had lost the sale. Some customers just won't wait. He visualized how Hiram was feeling right then: very bad. He decided not to mention it to Hiram. *He's being punished enough,* Bill guessed correctly.

By nine the entire sales force of Paramount Buick had shown up, including the latest addition, Ben Davis, who had come in at 8:55. It was his third day on the job. Bill had hired him with grave doubts. Ben seemed intelligent enough but moody and uncertain. His record showed five years of lackluster selling, two years in automobiles. To Bill, Ben seemed to lack the kind of toughness selling required. Still, he had seen more than one salesman suddenly come to life. Time would tell. He went back to his work.

It was a typical morning: his phone rang every five minutes or so, his service manager came in with problems, the accountant had matters to review. If he had one preoccupation, it was with his young salesman, Ben.

At about 10:15, Bill saw Ben go out the front door and drive away without saying a word to anyone. Concerned, Bill went to Ben's cubicle at once. He saw nothing unusual. Ben's umbrella still stood in the corner, and various books, manuals, and papers were on his desk.

Bill went back to his office. Hiram was busy on the phone as he walked by. "Good old Hi," he said. "Good and hungry and tough. Phones don't scare him one bit. Keeps calling till he hits." He wondered again where his youngest salesman had gone. "I'll give him a pep talk when he comes back," he said. For a moment, he wondered whether he would come back at all, but he dismissed the thought from his mind.

Ben Davis didn't come back that day or ever again. He left his umbrella to the next man who took over his cubicle.

◆◆◆◆

We have come to the end of three tales about salesmen, each capable, but each with contrasting real-time skills. Ben, with his habit of straying into imaginary "time," didn't even finish his day on the job. He wandered off, self-wounded and forlorn, his rescue awaiting an improved understanding of himself and his consciousness.

Hiram, wandering into imaginary "time," lost a sale but recovered, thanks more to his instinct for real-time work than to self-understanding.

But Bill, the self-made owner, was able to keep himself firmly in the *now*. This mastery of real time helps him get his work done and inspire others.

Staying in Real Time

—

POINTS TO REMEMBER

—

1. Real time is now.

2. Stay in real time as much as possible.

3. The past is a tool for learning, not for hurting yourself or others.

4. The future is for planning, not for the creation of anxiety or prophecy of doom.

5. The now is for doing. If you don't take advantage of the now, it will be gone in the blink of an eye.

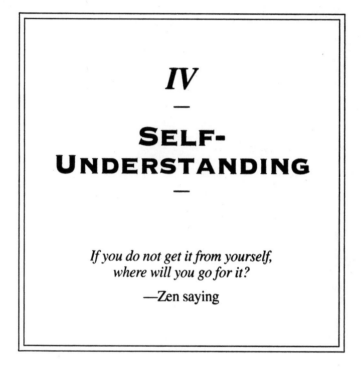

IV

—

SELF-
UNDERSTANDING

—

*If you do not get it from yourself,
where will you go for it?*

—Zen saying

11

—

HOW TO LOOK AT YOURSELF

—

Y ou have just left your home and are now in your car, heading for work. You are beginning another day of selling.

It so happens that you come nicely equipped with an intellect which is under your control and which is capable of many truly marvelous operations.

You can, among other things, see and hear, imagine and remember, think and know.

One of the most astonishing things you can do, however, is look at yourself while you are doing what you are doing.

Since you have this ability to be aware of yourself doing things, it may prove interesting, even useful, to put this ability to work.

Being aware of yourself is not something you must learn *how* to do, like learning how to do a spread-sheet on your computer. You already know how to be aware of yourself doing things, although you may seldom or indeed ever put this ability to work.

This ability is simply and only the activity of self-awareness, of being an observer of yourself while you are doing something, such as driving to work.

Here are three things that will happen should you decide to spend a little time using your self-awareness capability.

1. You will get to know yourself. As Yogi Berra once said, "You can see a lot just by looking." What you will see a lot of is yourself, since you are now targeting yourself. And you will learn a lot about yourself. Instead of having to rely on what others tell you about yourself (often erroneously), or on what you are able to recall about a past event in your life, you are now observing yourself in action as your own contemporary.

Say, for example, that you are trying to close a sale. The customer had just raised an objection that could ruin the sale if you cannot put it to rest immediately. You tense up because it is a serious objection that has killed previous attempts to get an order. This time, *because you are self-observing,* you smile rather than frown. Why? Because you are not compulsively thinking dire thoughts about saving the sale but are aware of yourself, aware that a reassuring smile from you will not only relax you but redirect the customer's attention from the thorn to the blossom. Your smile, timely and natural, springs from immediate self-awareness and could in itself save the sale. How? By a smile's power to transform the spirituality of the occasion, to change it from adversarial to friendly. You have used your intelligence, your Self-Observing (S-O) Function, to alter consciousness, to detoxify a situation by the meta-language of a genuine self-aware smile. You have also bought some time to meet the content of the objection, if necessary, which will now be easier for you to do.

2. You will find that you have, or actually *are,* a reality quite separate and distinct from the person who is doing things, such as selling or buying shoes. You will discover that there is a mysterious You who is "above the battle," an observer who is untouched and unharmed by anything good or bad that happens during a day of living and selling.

3. This knowledge of your separate reality will be a source of strength and comfort to you. And if you are ever tempted to doubt this knowledge, you can readily confirm it through your personal experience.

Looking at yourself in this way has a fancy name. It is called "meditation." But you must not be put off by the word, even though it may prompt you to think of monks sitting all day in their stalls or in their lotus positions or of adepts in India contemplating their navels. Let us, however, stick to the facts, which are as follows:

- You have the ability to look at yourself as someone in the act of driving a car, eating a piece of pie, and so forth.
- Looking at yourself while doing such things means that you are *watching* yourself doing things instead of just *doing* them.
- There is much to be learned from such self-awareness.
- "Meditation" is just a fancy name for a very natural,

very useful human capability. Meditation is
performed in monasteries but can be done anywhere,
privately and without cost or effort.

The question now is: Can looking at yourself in this way
make you a better, happier, more successful salesperson?

The answer is: If you find it useful to activate your S-O
Function, there can be no law against it. If, on the other hand,
it proves not very useful, you can always turn off the S-O
Function on your computer and go back to doing things the
old way.

More than likely, however, activating your ability to see
yourself in the very act of doing things will keep you from
getting into a rut and show you when, why, and how to correct mistakes. It can also cheer you up as you observe yourself doing things well. Thus, it can serve as a powerful tool
for self-improvement.

But there is a bigger payoff from being aware of yourself
as an observer of your own activity, particularly once this
practice has been established as a habit. Self-awareness
enables you to occupy at will the High Ground of Selfhood,
and thus keep events, however troubling, in perspective. It
will help you to fret and worry less about the unavoidable setbacks in life, and to maintain your cool and your sense of
humor when things look bleak or go bad.

Is there a real You that reveals itself in self-observation?

Yes, there is. It is easily discovered, but it can be missed
for an entire lifetime.

for an entire lifetime.

Finding the real You is easy, once you know it's there.

It is a wiser, saner, more benevolent self, a hidden resource waiting to be discovered.

It is the core of self-understanding and the supreme vantage point for true self-discovery.

In the next chapter we will focus on another mental activity that is in sharp contrast to looking at oneself.

It is the mind revisiting its past in an activity called "self-replay." Unlike looking at yourself *while* you are doing things, this activity is retrospective and after-the-fact. With self-replay you have to remember what you did and how it *was* (past tense), not how it *is* (present tense), as in self-observation.

12
—
SELF-REPLAY
—

Y ou are in a sales meeting, and you say what seems justified to you. You make a clear, heartfelt, blunt statement about how you perceive your company. You even name names.

You are angry but show restraint, given the circumstances. You have some long-standing complaints. It so happens that you are also exhausted after a long, hard road trip, and you are worried about your wife, who lately has not been well.

That night, when you are at home and in bed, you replay the sales meeting in your mind—not just once, but many times. the replaying torments you, and sleep will not come without a sedative.

Your replay is defective, and necessarily so. You are human, and not a TV camera calling up a tape. Your replay is a fictional reality. And just like Plato's prisoners in the cave, recounted in his book *The Republic,* you have mistaken shadows for the real thing. And you suffer just as the prisoners did.

Self-replay is not difficult.

Vast numbers of humans engage in it.

We look back endlessly at what we did, what we said, how we felt. It is easy to do, and it takes only an instant.

It is the self instantly replaying itself on the screen of memory.

A replay in the living, human memory is not the mechanical replay of the TV tape, however. The tape only "coughs up" what is captured; it cannot do otherwise.

Not so with our self-replay. We can and do amend and edit what we remember. We are witnesses, not documents; we render opinions, not records.

Say you were on the threshold of making a major sale when, suddenly, you lost it. The customer called you on the phone and announced that he had decided not to place the order with you. You tried to save it but met a stone wall of resistance. The memory of that missed opportunity, which seemed a sure thing and which would have made your year, haunts you. What did you do wrong? Why did the customer turn away at the last minute after many meetings and two friendly—and expensive—dinners with him and his wife? Did you unknowingly offend him? Or perhaps her? Did he suddenly get a better price from a competitor? Did somebody higher up kill the sale? You replay the affair, agonizing over it again and again. You finally come to the conclusion that the joke you told during the second dinner killed the sale. It was a bit coarse and, while he laughed heartily, his wife did not, though she remained cordial to you for the rest of the meal. Yes, that was it: the joke. The wife was offended, and that killed it. Spouses can do that. You imagined their conversasation later in bed: "Darling, do you really want to do business with that insensitive animal who goes around telling crude jokes to other men's wives? I was not amused. To me it was a slap in the face, and I want you to have no further dealings with him, that is, if you really love me."

You could not know that the wife had nothing to do with it. You lost the sale because your would-be buyer had a sudden offer from another company and had told no one. The sale was taken from you; you made no blunder, unless it was to count your chickens before they hatched.

We tend to trust our own replays. This is because they are self-produced and self-experienced, meaning we are twice implicated.

Self-replaying can be a profoundly useful and constructive capability.

Errors can be avoided, surely, if they can be recalled accurately. But the recall or replay is not the factual event as it happened; it is a mental construct, full of embellishment, with vast potential for error and misjudgment.

Our achievements can encourage us, of course, when we remember them.

Had we no memories, particularly no ability to self-replay, our lives would be closer to the enviable, unanguished lives of animals. Brute animals have no powers of self-replay, and thus no mood swings. Fido can always be depended on to remain himself: affectionate, loyal, and true. His is a narrow spectrum of steady, predictable behavior set by instinct. We cannot ascribe virtue to him, since he is only capable of being the "good dog" he has been bred and trained to be.

Our superior powers as humans involve dangers. The exercise of memory can be misused and produce disabling and destructive results, particularly when what we reconstruct in our replays demoralizes us and causes us to blame ourselves for events over which we really had no control.

That is why, without being smug or complacent, we should give ourselves the benefit of the doubt about our replays. And sometimes it may be better to engage in no replay of a given event, lest we wound ourselves unjustly and unnecessarily, as the anecdote above demonstrates.

Sometimes it is better to walk away from a failure to close a sale or to keep an old customer, however "sure" it was, because its "recapture" misleads us, often seriously.

One way to do this is by realizing the necessary defectiveness of any self-replay.

Present time, once lived, cannot be recaptured the way it was. For one thing, your emotions at the time were real, but the memory of them is a construct, that is, disembodied and shadowy.

Another way to deal with failure is through an unshakable understanding that the act of self-replaying is not automatic. You have to instigate it, "push the button" that calls up the replay. What comes up on the "screen" of the mind is *chosen. Selected.*

This point is not trivial.

You may ask, "If my self-replays are freely chosen and defective, why are they such a fixture in my life?"

The primary reason is your inescapable self-involvement, which prompts your interest in recapturing past memories and emotions. Another reason is the ease of recall.

The truly wise person, however, is not tempted by such reasons. He or she realizes that much of life's difficulties stem from the habit of replaying the past.

The replay of the sale that you "goofed," which is still burning in your mind, can add nothing to your paycheck and, in fact, may end up costing you a good deal more than money, unless you are careful. Careful? Yes, careful about letting any particular replay—or any group of them—dishearten or demoralize you. You are under no obligation to self-wound, to "pay" for your blunders with self-torturing replays, however fresh they may be in your consciousness.

Following the strategies in this book will empower you to walk away from any supposed blunder and start anew.

Like the referee at a sports event, you must be aware when you are in replay. For, even though a TV replay cannot lie or edit what the camera caught, it can "err" in the sense of missing a critical angle or focus.

The self-replay, alas, does not announce itself with some automatic signal, some red light on the set, and you can easily mistake it for the primary event.

Clearly, it is dangerous to "get lost" in your self-replay because you can easily mistake it for the real event. The memory of what happened on the phone or at the door of a potential customer is but a pale relic of the event in all its lived reality. Neither you nor your potential customers are abstractions, revisitable in the mind. There can be no dependable replay of your weariness at the end of the day, nor of your distraction over a sick child, a bank overdraft, a matrimonial concern. You cannot remember how anything *really was* without distortion and error.

This means that the self-replay can be taken with a grain of salt, and even dismissed as irrelevant if it discourages or demoralizes you.

There is no denying, however, that replays can be very valuable when used to learn and to grow, that is, when done strategically. Experience teaches. But since time spent in self-replay cuts into available time in the present, self-replay should be made to "pay" for itself with proportionate benefits. This is only fair. The benefits include maintaining self-esteem by learning and gaining encouragement from our past experiences. But they are not automatic; they must be shrewdly harvested, and shrewdness, as always, requires knowledge.

What knowledge, specifically?

Again, the knowledge that self-replays are mental constructs and must be actively perceived as such if one is to be safe from a "bad angle" or "bad focus."

Replay yourself, if you will.

But not because you must.

"Life is difficult," reads the opening line of the book *The Road Less Traveled* by M. Scott Peck.

Must life be difficult?

No, though it can be for those individuals who use their

self-replay abilities carelessly and wound themselves unnecessarily in the process. And this brings us to the subject of the next chapter: self-wounding.

13

—

SELF-WOUNDING

—

Y ou have just come from the office of the company president. You not only failed to get his signature on a contract, but you also succeeded in displaying publicly your shaky grasp of certain important facts and figures.

You have now reached your car and realize that you have locked yourself out of it.

You tell yourself loudly that you are stupid.

But you are not content to savage yourself once. No, you keep it up, adding scorn to self-contempt in a determined effort to convince yourself that your stupidity, attested to by your sales performance of the past hour and now symbolized by the locked door of your car, is profound and irremediable.

If the two experiences pain you, it comes as no surprise: you have been calling yourself "stupid" for some time. Now you are "sold."

This is an exorbitant price to pay for a sales encounter with a classic "window-shopper" who, unbeknownst to you, had boned up on engineering trivia in order to play with you a little, and for being a little absent-minded with your keys.

Clearly, your mental "immune system" isn't doing its job,

which is to protect you from assaults or threats to your self-respect and general well-being.

Does that include any attacks delivered by yourself as well?

It does. An assault on yourself of this nature and intensity is bad news. One attack from yourself, given your self-identification, is serious. After all, who can get closer to yourself than you? Where can you go to hide from yourself?

You have gone from a no-win selling situation and a blunder with your car keys to "locking yourself out" of your natural capacity—and your right—to self-esteem.

You have engaged in self-wounding, and you need to stop it before things get out of hand.

Out of hand?

Yes. For one thing, your self-view of being stupid will not stay shut up in your mind. Soon your immune system will get the message and slacken as a primary defense against disease. Your nervous, digestive, and vascular systems will quickly follow suit. This is called being "sympathetic" to higher orders and is addressed in my book *Perish the Thought: The Stress Connection,* coauthored by Herman M. Lubens, M.D.

Your self-view will also affect your morale and even your will to live.

You need to be rescued from your sorry opinion of yourself, and quickly.

This can best be done by you because, after all, you are (a) the culprit here, (b) the one most interested in stopping this self-wounding, and (c) the one who would most benefit from so doing.

But how? How do you prevent your self-wounding?

The first thing you can do is conform yourself to the facts.

The first fact is that you didn't get a sale from a "window-shopper" who deliberately tried to embarrass you. The second fact is that you locked yourself out of your car.

Neither of these facts documents your stupidity, only the fact that, like all mortals, you are capable of doing stupid things, in this case wasting your precious time on arrogant window-shoppers, and not carrying a spare key with you.

Another thing that you can do is to appreciate what an occasional blunder can do to humanize you, making you more tolerant of the blunders of others.

Still another is to refrain from thinking toxic thoughts such as your "stupidity."

Finally and perhaps most important, you can activate your ability to self-observe so that you may never again waste time with idle window-shoppers or lock yourself out of your car. But, if you ever again do so, you will at least know how to keep from wounding yourself.

14

—

BLAMING

—

The woman whom you put here with me—
she gave me fruit from the tree, and so I ate it.

—Adam, *Genesis* II, 12

T wo men are on their way by car to a crucial business meeting. They had flown in the day before, risen early at their hotel, ate breakfast, and jumped into their rental car with an hour to spare. A lucrative contract for the company they co-own needs only their attendance and their signatures.

Misadventure overtakes them. At an intersection their car collides with another car, sufficient to bring the police and an ambulance to the scene. It is two hours before the two men, shaken up but otherwise unhurt, are allowed to proceed.

They hurry on to the meeting only to learn that, because of their tardiness, the contract had been awarded by default to a rival company.

The two men are bitterly disappointed and seek relief by engaging in self-replays over lunch. Their dialogue is as follows:

Duncan, the driver (sheepishly): I had the right-of-way, Charley. We arrived first at that intersection. It was my very first accident in 22 years of driving.

Charley, the passenger (testily): You sure picked a bad time to have an accident. What was the big rush at that intersection, anyway? We had plenty of time. Besides, I don't think we had the right-of-way. Now we've lost our one big shot at expansion. You remind me of the football player who tried to run with the ball before he caught it. A little concentration by you at that intersection, and we'd have that contract in our pocket right now.

Duncan (defensively): Well, I'm not used to driving on only three hours of sleep. I wanted to turn in at eleven but, no, you had us up till three, reviewing everything. Getting your damned "ducks lined up," as you put it. So, if I'm to blame for losing this contract, you made a distinct contribution.

Charley (dogmatically): We got shot down at that intersection, Duncan, and you were at the wheel. I would have been happy to drive, but you got into the driver's seat. Remember?

Duncan (triumphantly): That was because I signed the rental agreement on the car.

Charley (petulantly): I wish to God now you hadn't. We had that contract all wrapped up. All we had to do was show up and it was ours. I don't know how I'm going to explain this to Jane. Your wife won't like it either.

◆◆◆◆

H ere we see blame being assigned, and it is done, typically, with replays tailored to accuse and to excuse.

Blaming satisfies the human need to address actions, to rescue these actions from brute, mindless forces of nature, and to provide an answer to the question, "Why did this happen?" Blaming also fulfills the need to pay a kind of guilt-tribute to the powers-that-be for impieties of inattention and stupidity.

"You are stupid" and "I am stupid!" spring too readily to human lips not to have some role or function as mantra or incantation. Yet the reluctance to blame has much to recommend it.

In the Babemba tribes of southern Africa, when a person acts unjustly or selfishly, he or she is placed in the center of the village. Everyone in the village then gathers around the accused in a large circle. Then, one after another, each villager, regardless of age, mentions all the good things the accused has done in life. Every good deed and word, every positive quality is recited at length and in a loud voice. No one may speak a single word of rebuke or criticism during the ceremony. Also, no falsehood, exaggeration, or facetiousness is permitted.

The ceremony does not end until everyone has exhausted

every positive remark about the person standing alone and unfettered in the circle.

When it is over, a joyous celebration ensues and the person is welcomed back into the tribe from which symbolically he or she has been separated.

This ceremony is the only method used by the Babembas to enforce morally acceptable behavior by members of the tribe. It has been found to strengthen a wrongdoer's self-image, helping him or her to live up to expectations of tribal members.

Is there a lesson here for the salesperson? There is.

Blaming yourself or others for any failure to achieve your selling goals is to focus on the thorns and to hide the blossom.

It is to abandon strategies that, steadily applied, will bear fruit in favor of idle gestures that waste time and drain energy for profitable activity. It is to exercise yourself, like Charley and Duncan, in rituals that overcome no objections and write no orders.

You will make mistakes in the hard, challenging business of trying to convince others to buy what you are selling. Some of these mistakes are truly unavoidable.

But as long as you do not make the major mistake of blaming others or circumstances for your mistakes, you will still be on the road to sales success. For you will not be mistaking the thorns for the blossom of yourself or of your product.

And there is a fatal error that you must avoid.

It is the error of self-blaming, a widespread and self-destroying practice. There can be no justification for it either in the contents of the self-replay or in what self-observation discerns.

Thorns, no doubt, are a fact of every salesperson's working life.

But the blossom is also there.

Selling the blossom is the ultimate intellectual strategy.

Self-Understanding

—

POINTS TO REMEMBER

—

1. It's okay to let people observe you in action, but why let them have all the fun? Do a little *self*-observation. You may like it. Then again, you may not. Since you operate the switches of your own consciousness, reach up and turn off your self-observation switch at your discretion.

2. I call self-observation "instant self-replay." This is accurate because (a) it can be done in an instant, (b) you are doing it and, (c) your are replaying how it was.

3. (a) and (b) are safe, but (c) can be a real problem because how it was is not equivalent to how it is, meaning that all self-replays are constructs; that is, they are not the real thing.

4. Self-replays can mislead. Because self-replays can mislead, they can be dangerous. Be warned!

5. Don't replay anything unless it serves your best interests, one of which is to learn from the past.

6. The universe is so entwined and interconnected that blaming becomes a useless exercise.

7. Beware of your worst critic, a person who will ultimately blame you for everything: yourself. You're only human, so cut yourself some slack.

—
CONCLUSION
—

I f you conclude as a consequence of reading *BrainSell* that the work of selling is a true profession, like law, medicine, journalism, engineering, or investment banking, one of my goals in writing this book will have been reached.

I had two additional goals.

My second was to convince you that there are four strategies—I call them "intellectual"—which have the potential to turn the world of selling into your own oyster, with a big, fat, flawless pearl inside.

My third goal was to show you, concretely and practically, how to open the oyster.

How did we get from blossoms and thorns to oysters?

You have an intellect. You figure it out.

Vaya con Dios.

INDEX

About the Author

John Cantwell Kiley, M.D., Ph.D., sees the sales profession from a broad perspective: *"Everything must go piggly-wiggly to market,"* as the poet Robert Frost reminds us. Yet, Kiley writes about selling concretely and practically, giving "bottom-line" advice to the workaday salesperson. In so doing he gives the selling profession its full due as a cornerstone of American life. Dr. Kiley has been president of two corporations, a university professor, and is, as he bills himself, an "Intellect Shock Therapist,"—on the lecture circuit. He is the author of a number of highly-acclaimed books, including *Self-Rescue*. He has always considered himself, proudly, a salesman.